100 facts

INVENTIONS

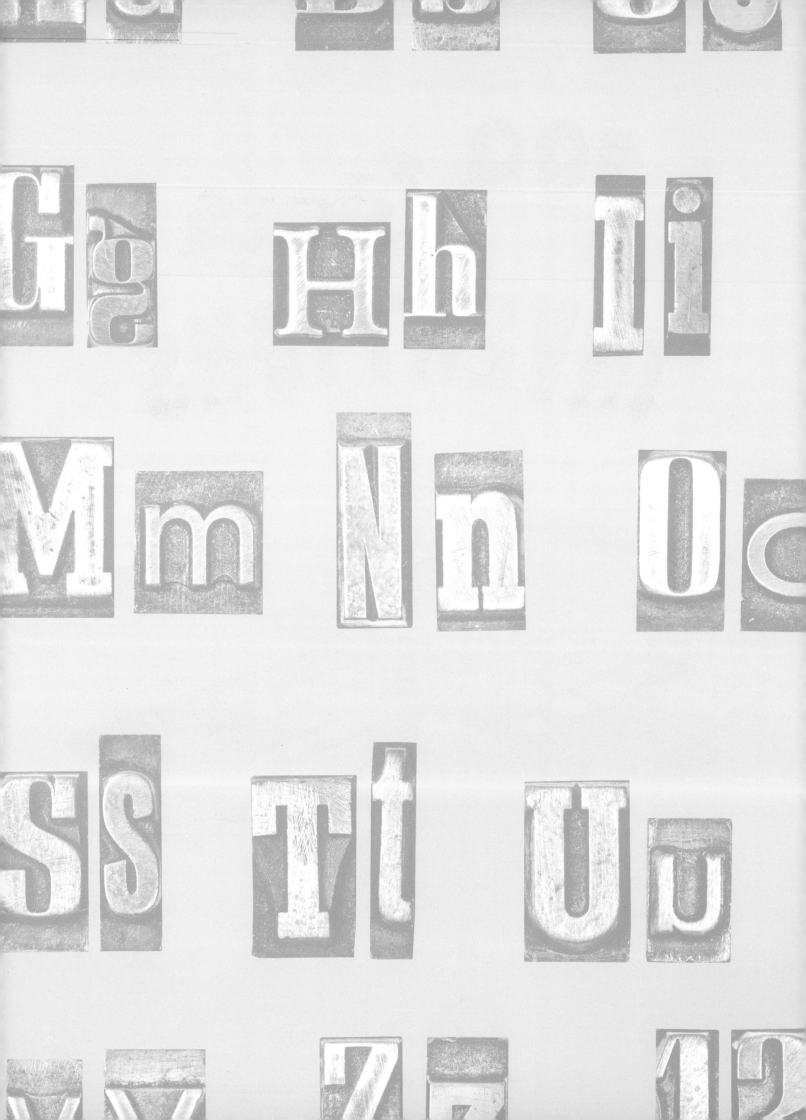

100 facts
INVENTIONS

Duncan Brewer

Consultants: Barbara Taylor and Steve Parker

Miles Kelly

First published in 2003 by Miles Kelly Publishing Ltd
Harding's Barn, Bardfield End Green, Thaxted, Essex, CM6 3PX, UK

This edition updated and printed in 2012

2 4 6 8 10 9 7 5 3

Publishing Director Belinda Gallagher
Creative Director Jo Cowan
Editorial Director Rosie McGuire
Designer Kayleigh Allen
Production Manager Elizabeth Collins
Reprographics Stephan Davis, Thom Allaway, Lorraine King
Assets Lorraine King

ISBN 978-1-84810-628-4

Printed in China

British Library Cataloguing-in-Publication Data
A catalogue record for this book is available from the British Library

ACKNOWLEDGEMENTS
The publishers would like to thank the following sources for the use of their photographs:
Key: t = top, b = bottom, c = centre, l = left, r = right, m = main, bg = background

Cover (front) Arsgera/Fotolia, (back) Caitlin Mirra/Shutterstock
Fotolia 8–9(tc) Alexey Khromushin; 14(b) Rafa Irusta; 25(b), 33(cr), 35(t), 36(cl), 3(tl), 47(tr) Sharpshot; 41(br) scazza;
46(tl) U.P. images **iStock** 18–19(bg) Sander Kamp; 27(br) Duncan Walker; 38(br) HultonArchive; 42(tl) hohos;
42(bl) James Steidl **NASA** 46(br) NASA Marshall Space Flight Center (NASA-MSFC); 47(bl) NASA Stennis Space Center;
47(br) NASA MSFC **Rex** 37(c)
Shutterstock 8–9(bg) Mark Carrel; 9(cr) Richard Peterson; 9(br) Fedorov Oleksiy; 10(tr) Marijus Auruskevicius;
11(tr) Maksym Gorpenyuk; 13(tl) Bernd Juergens; 13(br) Michael Stokes; 15(b) Orientaly; 17(br) Julija Sapic;
19(c) Oleg - F; 19(r) Kjersti Joergensen; 21(br) Darren Baker; 22(tl) Irafael; 23(tr) Thirteen; 24(l) Alex Staroseltsev;
27(bl K. L. Kohn; 28(t) Awe Inspiring Images; 29(c) Galushko Sergey; 29(bc) Indigo Fish; 29(tr) Ispace; 30(bl) Geoffrey
Kuchera; 31(t) Alexandru Chririac; 33(tl) marekuliasz; 33(bl) Lim Yong Hian; 34(tl) alexnika; 35(m) Caitlin Mirra; 36(violas)
Milan Vasicek; (conductor) HitToon.com; 37(br) Stephen Meese; 38(l) EW CHEE GUAN; 38(cr) Barry Barnes;
38(b) Pakhnyushcha; 39(br) Alexandr Kolupayev; 40–41(m) Becky Stares; 41(tr) c.; 43(cl) Gordan; 43(bl) drfelice;
45(t) Maksym Bondarchuk; 45(bl) steamroller_blues; 45(br) Slaven; 46–47(bg) plavusa87

All other photographs are from:
Corel, digitalSTOCK, digitalvision, John Foxx, PhotoAlto, PhotoDisc,
PhotoEssentials, PhotoPro, Stockbyte

All artworks are from the Miles Kelly Artwork Bank

Every effort has been made to acknowledge the source and copyright holder of each picture.
Miles Kelly Publishing apologises for any unintentional errors or omissions.

Made with paper from a sustainable forest

www.mileskelly.net
info@mileskelly.net

www.factsforprojects.com

Contents

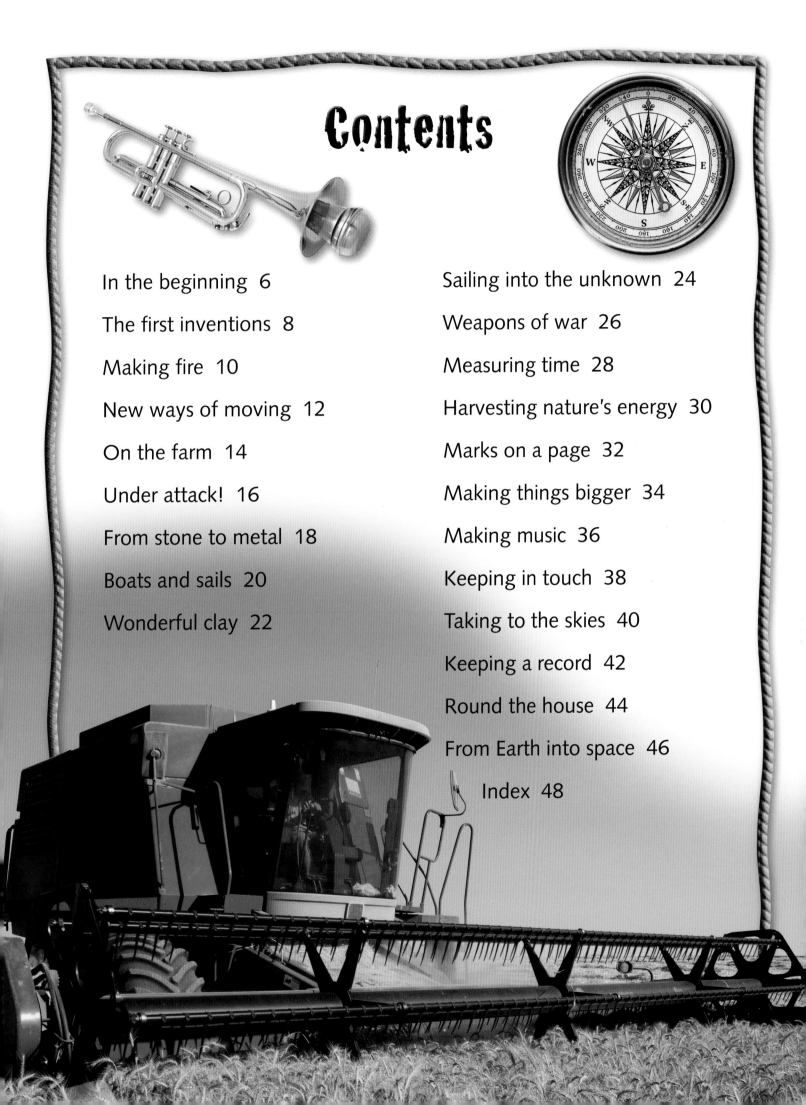

In the beginning

1 Humans have always been inventors. More than one million years ago, our ancient relatives made simple stone tools. Around 30,000 years ago our more recent ancestors were much more skilled at tool-making (1) and they had worked out how to sew skins together to make clothes (2). The first musical instruments were made from bone more than 20,000 years ago (3). Early humans lived by hunting animals, and invented bows and arrows to which they added tips of sharp stone. Tools, clothes, weapons, dwellings and other inventions gradually became more complicated and numerous.

▶ Stone Age clothes were made out of animal skins sewn together using a bone needle.

The first inventions

2 The first inventors lived about 2.5 million years ago. They were small, human-like creatures who walked upright on two legs. Their first inventions were stone tools. They hammered stones with other stones to shape them. These rough tools have been found in Tanzania in Africa. Scientists call this early relative of ours 'handy man'.

Spear made from wood with tip of sharp flint

3 Stone Age people made really sharp weapons and tools by chipping a stone called flint. They dug pits and tunnels in chalky ground to find the valuable flint lumps. Their digging tools were made from reindeer antlers.

▲ Flint tools were shaped to fit comfortably into the hand, with finely chipped cutting edges that could cut through large bones.

4 Early hunters were able to kill the largest animals. With flint tips on their weapons, they overcame wild oxen and horses and even killed huge, woolly mammoths. They used their sharp flint tools to carve up the bodies. The flint easily sliced through tough animal hides.

▼ Stone Age hunters trapped woolly mammoths in pits and killed them with spears and stones.

Stone

Pit covered with sticks

5 **The axe was a powerful weapon.** A new invention, the axe handle, made it possible to strike very hard blows. Fitted with a sharp stone head, the axe was useful for chopping down trees for firewood and building shelters.

▶ Axe heads were valuable, and were traded with people who had no flint.

MODERN AXE

▶ A modern axe is made of steel but it still has a long, sharp cutting edge and wooden handle.

▶ Saws were made from about 12,000 BC, and had flint 'teeth' held in place by resin.

MODERN SAW

▲ Today's steel saws also use many small sharp teeth to slice tough materials.

I DON'T BELIEVE IT!

Some Stone Age hunters used boomerangs! They made them out of mammoth tusks thousands of years before Australian boomerangs, and used them for hunting.

6 **Saws could cut through the hardest wood.** Flint workers discovered how to make very small flint flakes. They fixed the flakes like teeth in a straight handle of wood or bone. If the teeth broke, they could add new ones. Saws were used to cut through tough bones as well as wood.

Making fire

7 People once used fire created by lightning. The first fire-makers probably lived in East Asia more than 400,000 years ago. As modern humans spread from Africa, over 60,000 years ago, they found that northern winters were very cold, and fire helped them stay warm. They discovered how to twirl a fire stick very fast – by placing the loop of a bowstring around the stick and moving the bow back and forth. After thousands of years, people invented a way to make sparks from steel by hitting it with a flint. Now they could carry their fire-making tinderboxes around with them.

▲ People discovered that very hot flames would harden, or 'fire', pottery in oven–like kilns.

▶ Fire provided early people with warmth, light and heat to cook food. The temperature deep within a cave stays the same whatever the weather outside.

MAKING HEAT

When your hands are cold you rub them together. Do this slowly. They feel the same. Now rub them together really fast. Feel how your hands get warmer. Rubbing things together is called friction. Friction causes heat.

8 Fire makes food taste good. The invention of cooking made food safer, because cooking kills germs. Cooking roots and meat on a fire makes them more tender as well as tastier. Humans are the only animals that cook food.

▲ Some people like cooking outdoors on a fire, as our relatives did over a quarter of a million years ago.

9 Humans invented lamps to light deep, dark caves. The lamps were saucers of clay or stone that burned animal fat, with moss for a wick. Campfire flames kept wild animals away at night. They also cooked food and kept people warm. People could see to make wall paintings in the caves.

New ways of moving

10 With wheels you can move huge weights. Once, heavy weights were dragged along the ground, sometimes on sledges – parts of 7000-year-old sledges have been found in Scandinavia. Then, more than 5500 years ago, the Sumerians of Mesopotamia began to make wheels from carved planks, which they fastened together.

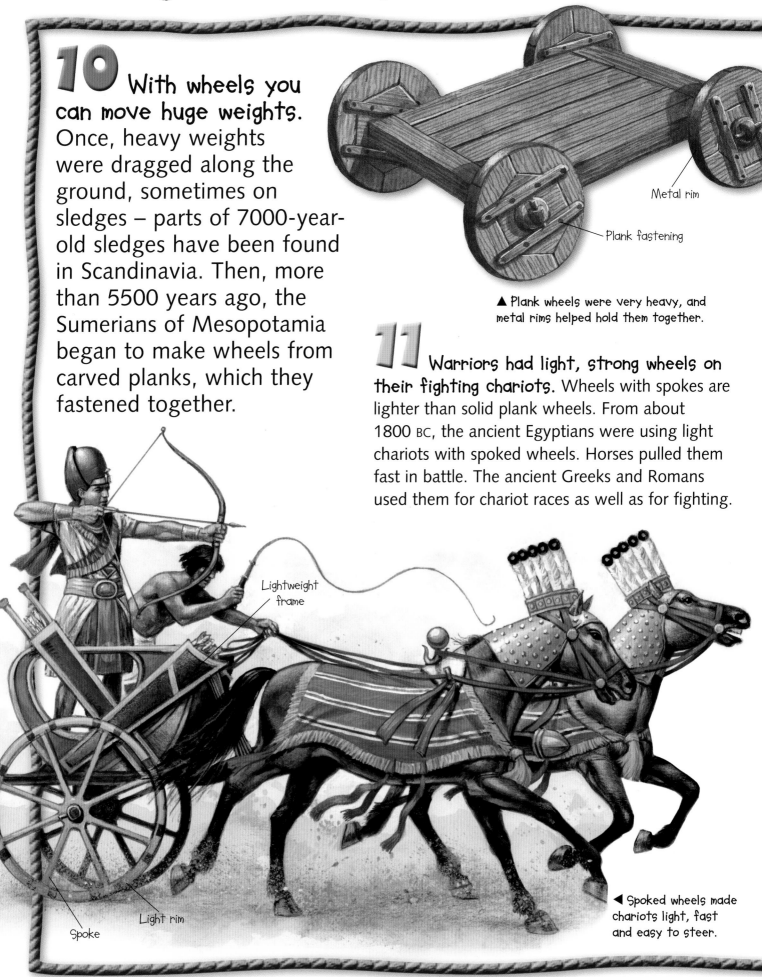

Metal rim

Plank fastening

▲ Plank wheels were very heavy, and metal rims helped hold them together.

11 Warriors had light, strong wheels on their fighting chariots. Wheels with spokes are lighter than solid plank wheels. From about 1800 BC, the ancient Egyptians were using light chariots with spoked wheels. Horses pulled them fast in battle. The ancient Greeks and Romans used them for chariot races as well as for fighting.

Lightweight frame

Spoke

Light rim

◀ Spoked wheels made chariots light, fast and easy to steer.

12 Railway lines were once made of wood! Wheels move easily along rails. Horses pulled heavy wagons on these wagonways over 400 years ago. William Jessop invented specially shaped metal wheels to run along metal rails in 1789. Modern trains haul enormous loads at great speed along metal rails.

▲ The first public railway opened in 1825 and was 40 kilometres long. A century later, steam trains like this puffed across whole continents.

QUIZ

Which came first?
1. (a) the chariot, or (b) the sledge?
2. (a) solid wheels, or (b) spoked wheels?
3. (a) rails, or (b) steam engines?

Answers:
1.b 2.a 3.a

13 In 1861, bikes with solid tyres were called boneshakers! An even earlier version of the bicycle was sometimes called the 'hobby horse'. It had no pedals, so riders had to push their feet against the ground to make it move. The invention of air-filled rubber tyres made cycling more comfortable.

▼ Wheels this size are usually only found on giant dump trucks. These carry heavy loads such as rocks or soil that can be tipped out.

14 Cars with gigantic wheels can drive over other cars! Big wheels give a smooth ride. At some motor shows, trucks with enormous wheels compete to drive over rows of cars. Tractors with huge wheels were invented to drive over very rough ground.

TIMELINE OF BICYCLE DESIGN

1818 — Hobby

1861 — Velocipede (Boneshaker)

Early 1870s — Penny Farthing

1976 — Mountain bike

▲ Bicycle design has come a long way — early designs were very heavy, and had no pedals or way of steering.

On the farm

15 The first farmers used digging sticks. In the area now called Iraq, about 9000 BC, farmers planted seeds of wheat and barley. They used knives made of flint flakes fixed in a bone or wooden handle to cut the ripe grain stalks. The quern was invented to grind grain into flour between two stones.

▲ Curved knives made of bone or wood were used for harvesting grain.

▼ Ploughed furrows made it easier to sow, water and harvest crops.

16 Humans pulled the first ploughs. They were invented in Egypt and surrounding countries as early as 4000 BC. Ploughs broke the ground and turned over the soil faster and better than digging sticks. Later on, oxen and other animals pulled ploughs. The invention of metal ploughs made ploughing much easier.

I DON'T BELIEVE IT!
Some Stone Age people invented the first fridges! They buried spare food in pits dug in ground that was always frozen.

17 For thousands of years, farming hardly changed. Then from about 300 years ago a series of inventions made it much more efficient. One of these was a seed-drill, invented by Englishman Jethro Tull. Pulled by a horse, it sowed seeds at regular spaces in neat rows. It was less wasteful than the old method of throwing grain onto the ground.

Side seed-box

Main seed-box

Coulter bar

▲ Jethro Tull's seed-drill sowed three rows of seed at a time.

18 Modern machines harvest huge fields of wheat and other crops in record time. The combine harvester was invented to cut the crop and separate grain at the same time. Teams of combine harvesters roll across the plains of America, Russia, Australia and many other places, harvesting the wheat. What were once huge areas of land covered with natural grasses now provide grain for bread.

19 Scientists are changing the way plants grow. They have invented ways of creating crop plants with built-in protection from pests and diseases. Other bumper crop plants grow well in places where once they could not grow at all because of the soil or weather.

▼ The latest combine harvesters have air-conditioned, soundproofed cabs and nearly all have sound systems. Some even use satellite navigation (satnav or GPS receivers) to plot their route automatically around fields.

Under attack!

▶ One end of the spear thrower is cupped to hold the spear butt.

20 Using a spear thrower is like having an arm twice the normal length. They were probably invented over 20,000 years ago. Hunters and warriors used them to hurl spears harder and farther than ever before. People all over the world invented this useful tool, and Australian Aborigines still use it.

21 Arrows from a longbow could pass through iron armour. Bows and arrows were invented at least 20,000 years ago. More than 900 years ago, the English longbow was made from a yew branch. Archers used it to fire many arrows a long distance in a short time. By law, all Englishmen had to practise regularly with the longbow. It helped them win many famous battles.

I DON'T BELIEVE IT!

Longbow archers could aim and fire six arrows per minute. The arrow sometimes went straight through an enemy's armour and out the other side.

▶ Bowmen often stood behind lines of sharpened stakes that protected them from enemies on horseback.

22 Crossbows had to be wound up for each shot. They were invented over 2000 years ago in the Mediterranean area, and fired a metal bolt or short arrow. They were powerful and accurate, but much slower than longbows. Soldiers used them in sieges throughout Europe from about AD 1000 onwards. But in battles, where speed was important, crossbows were often beaten by longbows.

▶ Crossbows were the first mechanical hand weapons, and at one time the Church tried to ban them.

23 In the Bible, David killed the giant, Goliath, with a pebble from a sling. The sling is an ancient weapon probably invented by shepherds. They used it when guarding their flocks, and still do in some countries. The slinger holds the two loose ends, and puts a pebble in the pouch. Then he whirls it round his head and lets go of one end. The pebble flies out at the target.

▼ Modern catapults with extra-strong rubber fling stones 200 metres or more.

24 Even a small catapult can do a lot of damage. The rubber strips are like bowstrings, which can fire a pebble from a pouch, like a sling. Some anglers use a catapult to fire food to attract fish to the water's surface.

From stone to metal

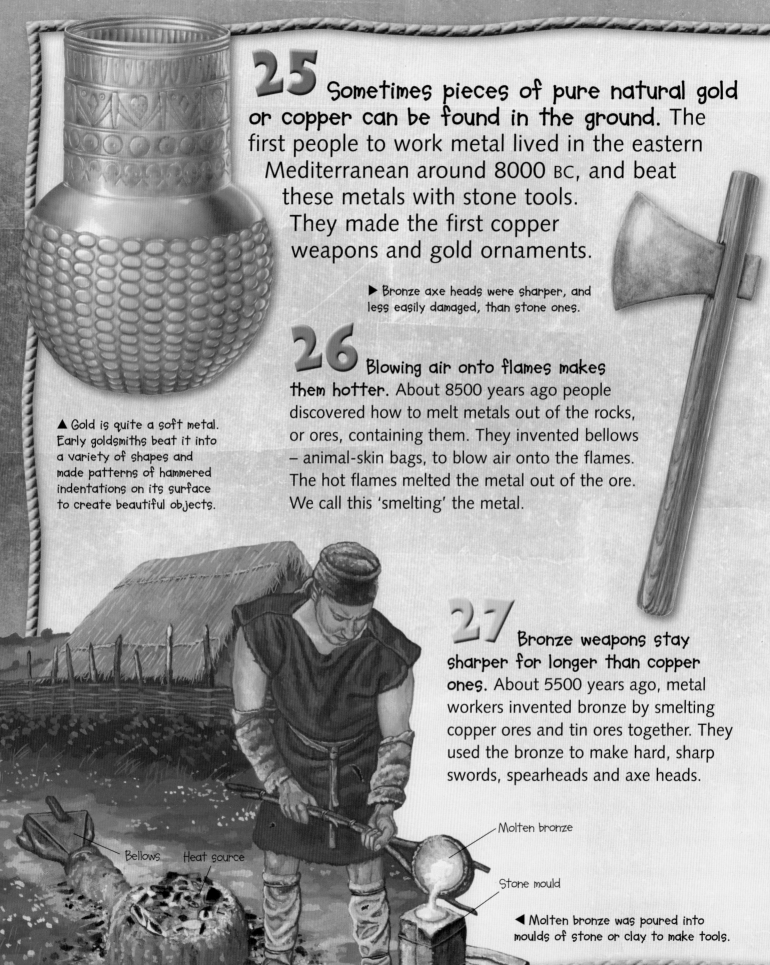

25 Sometimes pieces of pure natural gold or copper can be found in the ground. The first people to work metal lived in the eastern Mediterranean around 8000 BC, and beat these metals with stone tools. They made the first copper weapons and gold ornaments.

▶ Bronze axe heads were sharper, and less easily damaged, than stone ones.

▲ Gold is quite a soft metal. Early goldsmiths beat it into a variety of shapes and made patterns of hammered indentations on its surface to create beautiful objects.

26 Blowing air onto flames makes them hotter. About 8500 years ago people discovered how to melt metals out of the rocks, or ores, containing them. They invented bellows – animal-skin bags, to blow air onto the flames. The hot flames melted the metal out of the ore. We call this 'smelting' the metal.

27 Bronze weapons stay sharper for longer than copper ones. About 5500 years ago, metal workers invented bronze by smelting copper ores and tin ores together. They used the bronze to make hard, sharp swords, spearheads and axe heads.

Bellows   Heat source

Molten bronze

Stone mould

◀ Molten bronze was poured into moulds of stone or clay to make tools.

▲ After smelting, iron was beaten into shape to make strong, sharp weapons.

▲ Iron chains are made by hammering closed the red-hot links.

28 Armies with iron weapons can beat armies with bronze weapons. Iron is harder than bronze, but needs a very hot fire to smelt it. About 1500 BC, metal workers began to use charcoal in their fires. This burns much hotter than ordinary wood and is good for smelting iron.

29 The Romans were excellent plumbers. They made water pipes out of lead instead of wood or pottery. Lead is soft, easily shaped and is not damaged by water.

▼ At a smelting works metal ore is heated past its melting point and the liquid is poured to set in a mould.

30 Some modern steelworks are the size of towns. Steel is made from iron, and was first invented when small amounts of carbon were mixed into molten iron. Steel is very hard, and used to build many things, including ships and skyscrapers.

▶ Burj Khalifa in Dubai is the world's tallest building, at 829.8 metres. It has a steel framework weighing more than 4000 tonnes.

Boats and sails

31 Viking explorers reached America 1000 years ago. The world's first boats were log rafts, useful for carrying heavy loads, but very slow. Viking boats were fast, and could travel far across the open sea. Sails were invented at least 5000 years ago, and the Vikings used both sails and oars.

▶ Viking boats were made of long planks fitted onto wooden frames, and steered by means of a long oar fastened near the stern (back of the ship). They could be sailed across deep oceans, or rowed up shallow rivers, and made river journeys from the Baltic as far as the Black Sea.

I DON'T BELIEVE IT!

In 450 BC a merchant called Himilco sailed from North Africa to Britain. He ended up in Cornwall and bought Cornish tin!

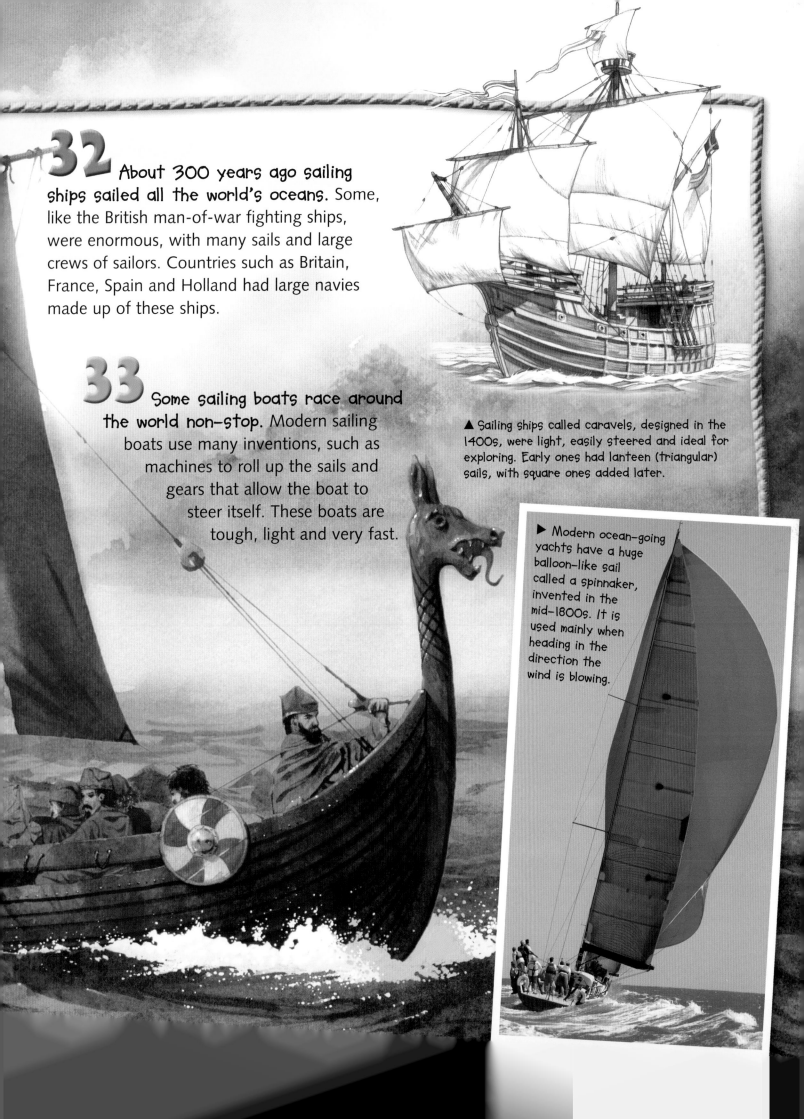

32 About 300 years ago sailing ships sailed all the world's oceans. Some, like the British man-of-war fighting ships, were enormous, with many sails and large crews of sailors. Countries such as Britain, France, Spain and Holland had large navies made up of these ships.

33 Some sailing boats race around the world non-stop. Modern sailing boats use many inventions, such as machines to roll up the sails and gears that allow the boat to steer itself. These boats are tough, light and very fast.

▲ Sailing ships called caravels, designed in the 1400s, were light, easily steered and ideal for exploring. Early ones had lanteen (triangular) sails, with square ones added later.

▶ Modern ocean-going yachts have a huge balloon-like sail called a spinnaker, invented in the mid-1800s. It is used mainly when heading in the direction the wind is blowing.

Wonderful clay

34 **Stone Age hunters used baked clay to do magic.** At least 30,000 years ago in Central Europe they discovered that some clay went hard in the sun, and even harder in a fire. They made clay figures of animals and humans, and used them in magic spells that they believed helped them catch food. Hardening clay in a fire was the start of the invention of pottery.

◀ By the year 500 AD in South America, Mayan craftsmen were 'firing' elaborate clay sculptures to make them hard and shiny.

Clay pot

Heat duct

Fuel

▶ Kilns produced much higher temperatures than open fires, and the heat could be controlled.

MAKE A COILED POT

Roll modelling clay into a long, 'snake' shape. Coil some of it into a flat circle. Continue to coil, building the coils upward. Try and make a bowl shape, and finally smooth out the ridges.

35 **Hard clay bowls changed the way people ate.** Early pots were made in China over 15,000 years ago. They were shaped by hand and hardened in fires. They could hold liquid, and were used to boil meat and plants. This made the food tastier and more tender. Around 7000 BC, potters in Southeast Asia used a new invention – a special oven to harden and waterproof clay, called a kiln.

36 Potters' wheels were probably invented before cart wheels. About 3500 BC in Mesopotamia (modern Iraq), potters invented a wheel on which to turn lumps of clay and shape round pots. By spinning the clay, the potter could make smooth, perfectly round shapes quickly.

▲ As the clay turns around on the disc 'wheel', the potter applies gentle pressure to shape it into a bowl, vase, urn or similar rounded item.

37 Brick-making was invented in hot countries without many trees. The first brick buildings were built in 9000 BC in Syria and Jordan. House builders made bricks from clay and straw, and dried them in the hot sun. By 3500 BC, bricks hardened in kilns were used in important buildings in Mesopotamia.

38 Modern factories make thousands of pots at a time. They are 'fired' in huge kilns. Wheels with electric motors are used, though much factory pottery is shaped in moulds. Teams of workers paint patterns.

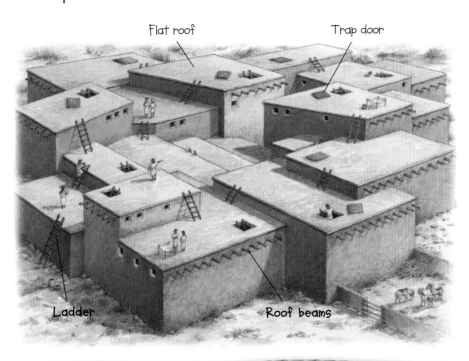

Flat roof

Trap door

Ladder

Roof beams

◄ With the invention of bricks, it was possible to construct large buildings. In 6000 BC, the Turkish town of Çatal Hüyük had houses with rooftop openings connected by ladders instead of doors.

Sailing into the unknown

39 Early sailors looked at the stars to find their way about. Around 1000 BC, Phoenician merchants from Syria were able to sail out of sight of land without getting lost. They knew in which direction certain stars lay. The north Pole Star, in the Little Bear constellation (star group), always appears in the north.

▲ Two stars in the Great Bear constellation are called the Pointers. They point to the north Pole Star in the Little Bear constellation.

40 Magnetic compasses always point north and south. They allow sailors to navigate (find their way) even when the stars are invisible. The Chinese invented the magnetic compass about 3000 years ago. It was first used in Europe about 1000 years ago.

◀ Compasses have a magnetized needle placed on a pivot so it can turn easily. Beneath this is a card with marked points to show direction.

41 Early maps showed where sea monsters lived. The first attempt at a world map was drawn by the Greek Ptolemy in AD 160. Greek maps of around 550 BC showed the known world surrounded by water in which monsters lived. Over 500 years ago, Pacific islanders had maps of sticks and shells, showing islands and currents. The first globe was invented in 1492 by a German, Martin Behaim.

▶ Using stick and shell maps, Pacific islanders successfully crossed thousands of kilometres of ocean.

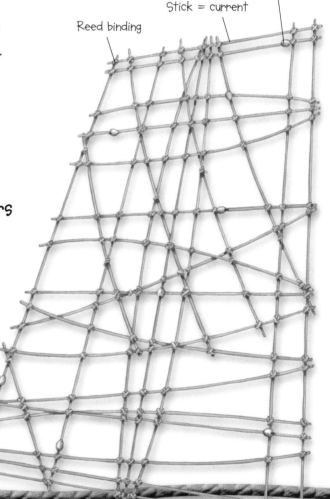

Shell = island
Stick = current
Reed binding

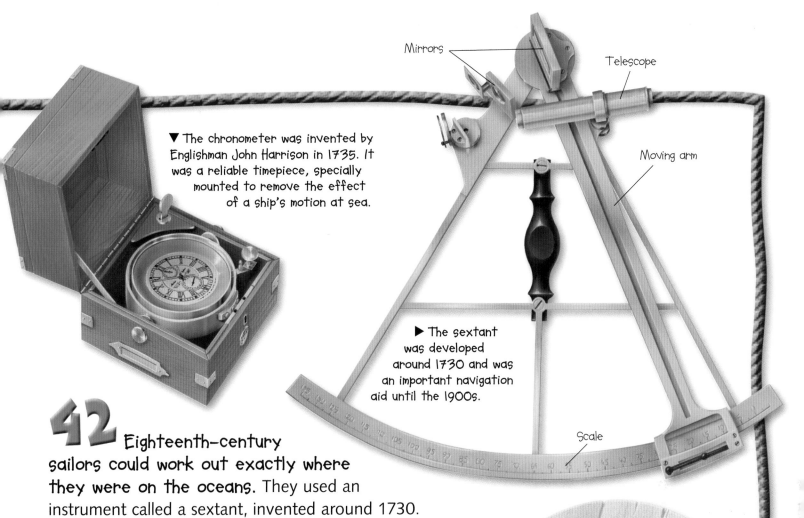

▼ The chronometer was invented by Englishman John Harrison in 1735. It was a reliable timepiece, specially mounted to remove the effect of a ship's motion at sea.

Mirrors

Telescope

Moving arm

▶ The sextant was developed around 1730 and was an important navigation aid until the 1900s.

Scale

42 Eighteenth-century sailors could work out exactly where they were on the oceans. They used an instrument called a sextant, invented around 1730. The sextant measured the height of the Sun from the horizon. The chronometer was an extremely reliable clock that wasn't affected by the motion of the sea.

USING A COMPASS

Take a compass outside and find out which direction is north. Put a cardboard arrow with 'N' on it on the ground pointing in the right direction. Then try to work out the directions of south, west and east.

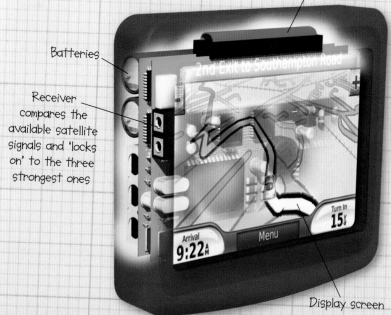

▼ Modern navigation instruments use signals from several satellites to pinpoint their position.

Antenna (aerial) detects signals from available satellites

Batteries

Receiver compares the available satellite signals and 'locks on' to the three strongest ones

2nd Exit to Southampton Road

Arrival 9:22ᴬᴹ

Menu

Turn In 15ᵧ

Display screen

43 New direction-finding inventions can tell anyone exactly where they are. A hand-held instrument, called a GPS receiver, receives signals from satellites in space. It shows your position to within a few metres. These receivers can be built into cars, ships, planes – even mobile phones!

Weapons of war

▶ Medieval sieges of well-protected forts or cities sometimes lasted for months.

Trebuchet

Siege tower

Battering ram

Ballista

44 The Romans invented massive rock-hurling weapons. In medieval times, armies in Europe and the Middle East still used the same weapons in city and castle sieges. The trebuchet slung great rocks or burning material over city walls. The ballista fired missiles such as stones or spears with huge force at the enemy.

45 The first gunpowder was used in fireworks. The Chinese invented gunpowder over 1000 years ago. In 1221 they used it to make exploding bombs and in 1282 they invented the first gun, a cannon. Cannons and mortars, which fired bombs or large stone balls very high through the air, were used in European sieges from the 14th century onwards. The first small firearms carried by soldiers appeared in the 15th century.

46 The battering ram could smash through massive city walls and gates. The Egyptians may have invented it in 2000 BC to destroy brick walls. It was a huge tree-trunk, often with an iron head, swung back and forth in a frame. Sometimes it had a roof to protect the soldiers from rocks and arrows from above.

47 Gunpowder was used in tunnels to blow up castle walls. Attackers in a siege dug tunnels under the walls and supported them with wooden props. Then, they blew up or burned away the props so that the walls collapsed.

48 Greek fire was a secret weapon that burned on water. The Greeks invented it in the 7th century AD to destroy ships attacking Constantinople. A chemical mixture was squirted at enemies through copper pipes. It was still being used many centuries later in medieval sieges, pumped down onto the heads of attackers.

▼ The biggest battleship guns can hurl explosive shells more than 40 kilometres.

▲ The Gatling gun could fire six bullets a second.

49 Modern machine guns can fire thousands of bullets per minute. Richard Gatling, an American, invented a gun that would later lead to the development of the machine gun in 1862. As in all modern guns, each machine-gun bullet has its own metal case packed with deadly explosives.

Measuring time

50 The huge stone slabs of Stonehenge can be used as a calendar. Some of its stones are lined up with sunrise on the longest day of the year. It was built and rebuilt in Wiltshire in southern England between 3000 and 1550 BC.

▶ A sundial's shadow moves from west to east during the day.

▼ Raising the huge main stones of Stonehenge required the muscles of many workers and the know-how of skilled Bronze Age engineers.

Hour markings

Shadow

Pointer

1862 - 1867

51 One of the earliest clocks was a stick stuck in the ground. Invented in Egypt up to 4000 years ago, the length and position of the shadow gave the time of day. Later sundials had a face with hours, and a pointer that cast a shadow.

52

Candles, water and sand can all be used to tell the time. The Egyptians invented a clock that dripped water at a fixed rate about 1400 BC. Candle clocks were marked with rings, and in the hourglass, invented about AD 1300, sand ran between two glass globes.

► An hourglass shows a time period has passed, not the time of day.

◄ Until the invention of quartz movements, wristwatches contained springs and cogs.

Gear wheel

Ratchet wheel

53

You can't see any moving parts in a modern quartz clock. Early clocks depended on movement. A Dutchman, Christiaan Huygens, invented a clock in 1656 which depended on a swinging pendulum. About the same time, clocks driven by coiled springs were invented. Modern quartz crystal clocks work on invisible vibrations and are very accurate. They were first produced in 1929.

54

Some clocks are like toys. Swiss cuckoo clocks contain a bird on a spring that flies out of a little door and 'cuckoos' the time. Some 18th-century clocks looked like ships, and their guns fired to mark the hours.

► Wristwatches were not made until 1790. Many modern watches have a liquid crystal display (LCD) and show changing numerals instead of hour and minute hands.

MAKE A SHADOW CLOCK

Fix about 60 centimetres of garden cane upright in a flat piece of ground. Use lollipop sticks or twigs to mark the length and position of the shadow every hour, from 9 a.m. to 4 p.m., if possible. Which hour casts the shortest shadow?

Harvesting nature's energy

55 The first inventions to use wind power were sailing boats. Invented around 3500 BC by the Egyptians, and also by the Sumerians of Mesopotamia, the first sailing boats had a single square sail. By AD 600, windmills for grinding grain had been invented in Arab countries. Some European windmills, in use from about AD 1100 onwards, could be turned to face the wind.

56 The first waterwheels invented were flat, not upright. The ancient Greeks were using upright wheels more than 2100 years ago, and the Romans improved the design with bucket-like containers and gears to slow the turning rate. As well as grinding corn, some were used to drive pumps or saws.

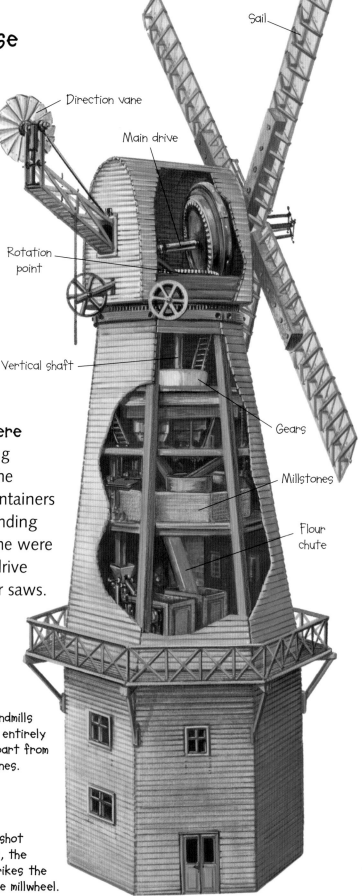

Sail

Direction vane

Main drive

Rotation point

Vertical shaft

Gears

Millstones

Flour chute

► Many windmills were made entirely of wood apart from the millstones.

◄ In overshot watermills, the water strikes the top of the millwheel.

I DON'T BELIEVE IT!

The earliest steam engine was totally useless. Around 2000 years ago a Greek engineer invented a steam machine with a spinning metal ball. Unfortunately no one could think of any use for it.

▲ Hydroelectric dams change the energy of moving water into electrical energy.

57 **Early steam engines often threatened to explode.** Thomas Savery's 1698 steam pump, invented in Devon, England, wasted fuel and was dangerous. Englishman Richard Trevithick developed a steam engine to move on tracks in 1804.

58 **Spinning magnets can create an electric current.** Michael Faraday and other scientists invented the first magnetic electricity generators (producers) in the 1830s. Today, huge dams use the power of millions of tonnes of flowing water to turn electricity generators, which have spinning electromagnets inside them.

59 **The strength of the wind usually increases the higher up you are.** Some of the largest wind turbines in use today stand as high as a 50-storey building, with propellers spanning more than the length of a football pitch. They produce enough electricity to power 5000 homes or more.

Generator changes the spinning movement from the rotor into electrical energy

The angle of the blades changes according to the speed of the wind

Yaw control pod swings around to keep the rotor blades pointing into the wind

▶ An increasing number of wind turbines are being built to make electricity.

Rotor blade

Marks on a page

Phoenician

Classical Greek

Roman

Cyrillic

Modern Hebrew

Modern Arabic

Ancient Egyptian

Chinese

Japanese

▲ Ancient picture writing used hundreds of different signs, but most modern alphabets have far fewer letters.

60 **The first writing was made up of pictures.** Writing was invented by the Sumerians 5500 years ago. They scratched their writing onto clay tablets. The most famous word pictures are the 'hieroglyphs' of ancient Egyptians from about 5000 years ago. Cuneiform writing was made up of wedge shapes pressed into clay with a reed. It followed the Sumerian picture writing.

▲ Some of the religious books handwritten by monks were decorated with beautiful illustrations.

61 **The world's earliest books were rolls of paper made from reeds.** The first of this kind was produced in Egypt between 1500 BC and 1350 BC and was called 'The Book of the Dead'. Christian monks used to write their religious books on sheets of parchment made from animal skins.

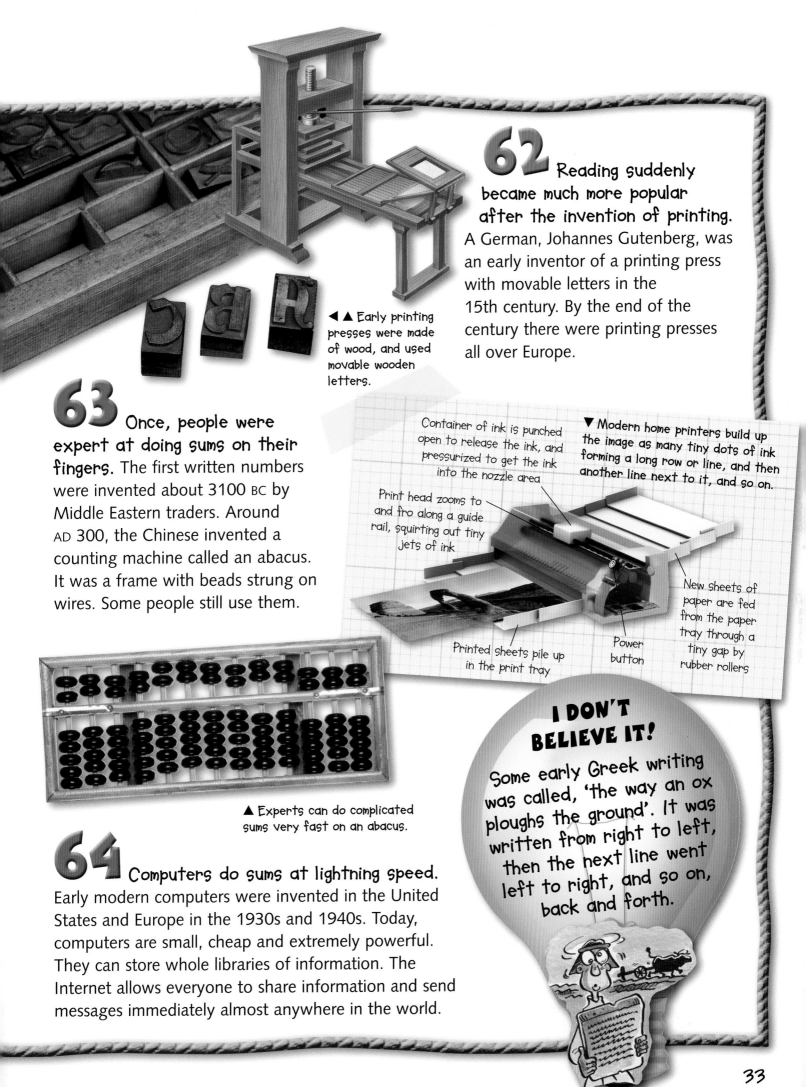

62 Reading suddenly became much more popular after the invention of printing. A German, Johannes Gutenberg, was an early inventor of a printing press with movable letters in the 15th century. By the end of the century there were printing presses all over Europe.

◀ ▲ Early printing presses were made of wood, and used movable wooden letters.

63 Once, people were expert at doing sums on their fingers. The first written numbers were invented about 3100 BC by Middle Eastern traders. Around AD 300, the Chinese invented a counting machine called an abacus. It was a frame with beads strung on wires. Some people still use them.

Container of ink is punched open to release the ink, and pressurized to get the ink into the nozzle area

▼ Modern home printers build up the image as many tiny dots of ink forming a long row or line, and then another line next to it, and so on.

Print head zooms to and fro along a guide rail, squirting out tiny jets of ink

New sheets of paper are fed from the paper tray through a tiny gap by rubber rollers

Printed sheets pile up in the print tray

Power button

▲ Experts can do complicated sums very fast on an abacus.

64 Computers do sums at lightning speed. Early modern computers were invented in the United States and Europe in the 1930s and 1940s. Today, computers are small, cheap and extremely powerful. They can store whole libraries of information. The Internet allows everyone to share information and send messages immediately almost anywhere in the world.

I DON'T BELIEVE IT!
Some early Greek writing was called, 'the way an ox ploughs the ground'. It was written from right to left, then the next line went left to right, and so on, back and forth.

Making things bigger

▲ Spectacles became important as more people began to read books.

65 **Small pieces of glass can make everything look bigger.** Spectacle-makers in Italy in the 14th century made their own glass lenses to look through. These helped people to read small writing. Scientists later used these lenses to invent microscopes, to see very small things, and telescopes, to see things that are far away.

66 **Scientists saw the tiny bacteria that cause illness for the first time with microscopes.** The Dutch invented the first microscopes, which had one lens. In the 1590s Zacharias Janssen of Holland invented the first microscope with two lenses, which was much more powerful.

◄ Early microscopes with two or more lenses, like those of English inventor Robert Hooke (1635–1703), were powerful, but the image was unclear.

67 **The Dutch tried to keep the first telescope a secret.** Hans Lippershey invented it in 1608, but news soon got out. Galileo, an Italian scientist, built one in 1609. He used it to get a close look at the Moon and the planets.

QUIZ
1. Which came first, (a) the telescope, or (b) spectacles?
2. Do you study stars with (a) a microscope, or (b) a telescope?
3. Which are smaller, (a) bacteria, or (b) ants

Answers:
1b 2b 3a

68 Modern microscopes make things look thousands of times bigger. A German, Ernst Ruska, invented the first electron microscope in 1933. It made things look 12,000 times their actual size. The latest microscopes can magnify things millions of times.

◄ An electron microscope shows a tiny parasite in monstrous detail, but this tick is actually less than 15 millimetres long.

69 You cannot look through a radio telescope. An American, Grote Reber, invented the first one and built it in his backyard in 1937. Radio telescopes pick up radio signals from space with a dish-shaped receiver. The signals come from distant stars, and, more recently, from space probes.

► Most radio telescope dishes can be moved to face in any direction.

Making music

70 Humans are the only animals that play tunes on musical instruments. Stone Age people made rattles and similar noise-makers from mammoth bones and tusks. Instruments you hit or rattle are called percussion instruments, and are still used in modern orchestras.

▼ The instruments of the modern orchestra are grouped into sections according to type – usually string, woodwind, brass and percussion.

GUIDE TO THE ORCHESTRA

■ **Percussion** instruments, such as drums, produce sound when they are made to vibrate by being hit, rubbed, shaken or scraped.

■ **Brass** instruments, such as horns, are made of curled brass tubes. Sound is produced by blowing into a cup-shaped mouthpiece.

■ **Woodwind** instruments produce sound when a player blows against an edge (as in flutes) or through a wooden reed (as in clarinets).

■ **String** instruments have strings. They produce sound when their strings are plucked or bowed.

71 Over 20,000 years ago Stone Age Europeans invented whistles and flutes. They made them out of bones or antlers. Modern flutes still work in a similar way – the player covers and uncovers holes in a tube while blowing across it.

72 The earliest harps were made from tortoise shells. They were played in Sumeria and Egypt about 5000 years ago. Modern harps, like most ancient harps, have strings of different lengths.

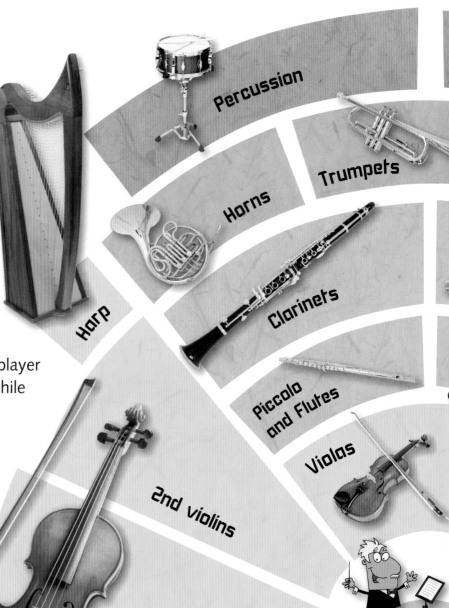

Percussion

Trumpets

Horns

Clarinets

Harp

Piccolo and Flutes

Violas

2nd violins

1st violins

Conductor

73 Pianos have padded hammers inside, which strike the strings. The first piano-like instrument was invented in about 1480 and its strings were plucked, not struck, when the keys were pressed. It made a softer sound than a modern piano.

▲ The grand piano's strings are laid out horizontally in a harp-shaped frame.

Timpani

Trombones

Tubas

Bassoons

Oboes

Double basses

Cellos

74 The trumpet is among the loudest instruments in the orchestra. A trumpet-like instrument was found in Tutankhamen's tomb in Egypt dating back to 1320 BC. Over 2000 years ago, Celtic warriors in northern Europe blew bronze trumpets shaped like mammoth tusks to frighten their enemies.

◀ The trumpet, played here by award-winning Alison Balsom, has a total tubing length of about 148 centimetres as well as three moveable valves.

75 Bagpipes sound as strange as they look. They were invented in India over 2000 years ago. The Roman army had bagpipe players. In the Middle Ages, European and Middle Eastern herdsmen sometimes played bagpipes while they looked after their animals.

▶ Some modern bagpipes still have a bag of sewn animal skins.

Keeping in touch

76 Some African tribes used to use 'talking drums' to send messages. Native Americans used smoke signals, visible several miles away. Before electrical inventions such as the telephone, sending long-distance messages had to be a simple process.

77 Wooden arms on tall poles across the country sent signals hundreds of miles in 18th-century France. Claude Chappe invented this system, now called semaphore, in 1797. Until recently, navies used semaphore flags to signal from ship to ship. In 1838 American Samuel Morse invented a code of short and long bursts of electric current or light, called dots and dashes. It could send messages along a wire, or could be flashed with a light.

◄ Skilled morse code operators could send 30 words per minute.

▼ Each position of the semaphore signaller's arms forms a different letter. What does this message say?

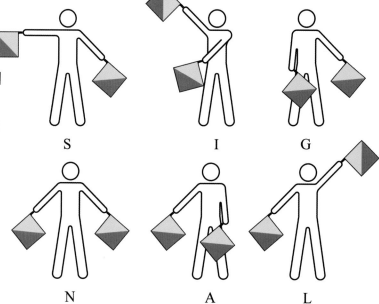

S   I   G

N   A   L

78 The telephone can send your voice around the world. A Scotsman, Alexander Graham Bell, invented it in the 1870s. When you speak, your voice is changed into electric signals that are sent along to a receiver held by the other user. Within 15 years there were 140,000 telephone owners in the United States.

Transmitter   Receiver

J.T.B. DEL.

► Bell's early telephone (top) in 1876 had one of the first electrical loudspeakers. The modern moving-coil design was invented in 1898 by Oliver Lodge.

▼ Smartphones have a touch-sensitive screen rather than buttons or keys.

Protective screen

Touch screen

Power button

Metal case

Small but powerful and long-lasting rechargeable battery

Sockets link the phone physically to a computer or network, to download or upload information

Uplink to telecom satellite

Downlink to hub

▼ The mobile network is divided into areas called 'cells', each with a receiver-transmitter mast, linked by combinations of wires, radio waves, microwaves, optical fibres and satellites.

Main hub

Person makes a call on cellphone A

Radio link to local mast

Person receives the call on cellphone B

79 With a mobile or cellphone you can talk to practically anyone wherever you are. Your voice is carried on radio waves or microwaves and passed from antenna to antenna until it reaches the phone you are calling. Some of the antennas are on space satellites.

80 Radio signals fly through the air without wires. An Italian, Guglielmo Marconi, invented the radio or 'wireless' in 1899. Radio stations send signals, carried on invisible radio waves, which are received by an antenna. A Scot, John Logie Baird, invented an early TV system in 1926. TV pictures can travel through the air or along wires.

I DON'T BELIEVE IT!

Early TV performers had to wear thick, clownlike makeup. The pictures were so fuzzy that viewers could not make out their faces otherwise.

▶ Live TV images can be beamed to a satellite in space, then redirected to the other side of the world.

TV camera

Taking to the skies

81 The first hot-air balloon passengers were a sheep, a duck and a cockerel. The French Montgolfier brothers invented the hot-air balloon in 1782. The first human passengers often had to put out fires, as the balloon was inflated by hot air created by burning straw and wool!

▲ The Montgolfier hot-air balloon made the first untethered, manned flight from Paris in 1783.

► The Wright Flyer had a spruce wood frame and canvas covering. It flew with the small wing at the front.

82 Many inventors have tried to fly by flapping birdlike wings. All have failed. One of the first bird-men crashed to his death at a Roman festival in the 1st century AD.

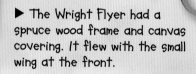

83 The first aircraft flight lasted just 12 seconds. The Wright brothers invented their airplane and flew it in 1903 in the United States. In 1909 a Frenchman, Louis Blériot, flew across the Channel. In World War I (1914–1918), airplanes were used in combat. In World War II (1939–1945), aircraft such as the British Spitfire beat off German air attacks.

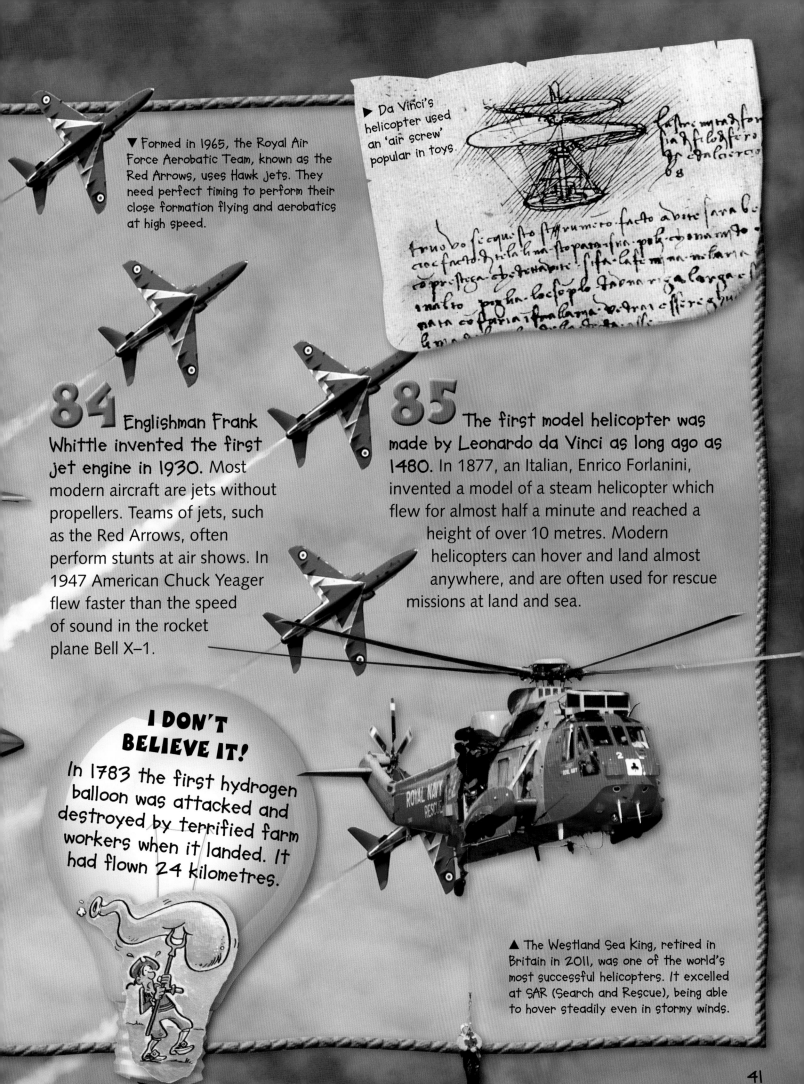

▼ Formed in 1965, the Royal Air Force Aerobatic Team, known as the Red Arrows, uses Hawk jets. They need perfect timing to perform their close formation flying and aerobatics at high speed.

▶ Da Vinci's helicopter used an 'air screw' popular in toys.

84 Englishman Frank Whittle invented the first jet engine in 1930. Most modern aircraft are jets without propellers. Teams of jets, such as the Red Arrows, often perform stunts at air shows. In 1947 American Chuck Yeager flew faster than the speed of sound in the rocket plane Bell X–1.

85 The first model helicopter was made by Leonardo da Vinci as long ago as 1480. In 1877, an Italian, Enrico Forlanini, invented a model of a steam helicopter which flew for almost half a minute and reached a height of over 10 metres. Modern helicopters can hover and land almost anywhere, and are often used for rescue missions at land and sea.

I DON'T BELIEVE IT!

In 1783 the first hydrogen balloon was attacked and destroyed by terrified farm workers when it landed. It had flown 24 kilometres.

▲ The Westland Sea King, retired in Britain in 2011, was one of the world's most successful helicopters. It excelled at SAR (Search and Rescue), being able to hover steadily even in stormy winds.

Keeping a record

▼ Thomas Edison produced many important inventions, including sound recording, electric light bulbs and an early film-viewing machine.

86 **The first sound recording was the nursery rhyme, 'Mary had a little lamb'.** In 1877 an American, Thomas Edison, invented a way of recording sounds by using a needle to scratch marks on a cylinder or tube. Moving the needle over the marks again repeated the sounds. Performers spoke or sang into a horn, and the sounds were also played back through it.

MODERN MUSIC PLAYER

▲ Digital music players can hold over two weeks of sound recording, played through earphones or a dock with speakers.

87 **To play the first disc records, you had to keep turning a handle.** Emile Berliner, a German, invented disc recording in 1887. The discs were played with steel needles, and soon wore out. They also broke easily if you dropped them. Long-playing discs appeared in 1948. They had 20 minutes of sound on each side and were made of bendy plastic, which didn't break so easily.

▼ Early record players had to be wound up between records, and the loudspeaker was a large horn.

QUIZ

1. Were the first recordings on (a) discs, or (b) cylinders?
2. Which came first, (a) movies, or (b) long-playing records?
3. Was the first photograph of (a) flowers, or (b) rooftops?
4. The first movies were viewed through a hole in a box — true or false?

Answers:
1.b 2.a 3.b 4.True

88
It took eight hours to take the world's first photograph in 1826. Frenchman Joseph Nicéphore Niépce was the inventor, and the first photograph was of rooftops. Early cameras were huge, and the photos were on glass plates. In 1881 Peter Houston invented rolls of film, which George Eastman developed for the company Kodak, making photography much easier.

▲ Digital cameras have a display screen that shows the view the lens sees, which is the image that will be stored.

89
Only one person at a time could watch the first movies. The viewer peered through a hole in a box. Thomas Edison's company invented movies in 1888. The invention of a projector in 1895 by the French Lumière brothers allowed a whole audience to watch the film on a screen.

▲ The Lumière brothers, who invented the movie projector, also made films and opened the first public cinema.

▶ Launched in 2001, the iPod took little more than one year to develop.

90
The forerunner of the MP3 player was the portable laser-based CD player. It was more than ten times bigger and heavier than an iPod. Moving it often made the compact disc (CD) skip.

Round the house

91 A horse and cart were needed to move the first successful vacuum cleaner around. An English engineer, Hubert Cecil Booth, invented it in 1902. The first 'Hoover' electric vacuum cleaner was built from a wooden box, an electric fan and an old sack in 1907 in America.

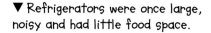
▼ Refrigerators were once large, noisy and had little food space.

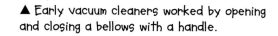
▲ Early vacuum cleaners worked by opening and closing a bellows with a handle.

92 Early refrigerators, invented in the 19th century, killed many people. They leaked the poisonous gas that was used to cool them. In 1929 the gas was changed to a non-poisonous one called freon. We now know that freon causes damage to the planet's atmosphere, so that has been changed too.

QUIZ

1. Did the first 'Hoover' need (a) a horse, or (b) an electric fan?

2. Were early refrigerators dangerous because (a) they blew up, or (b) they leaked poison gas?

3. The Cretans had china toilets 4000 years ago – true or false?

Answers:
1.b 2.b 3.False

44

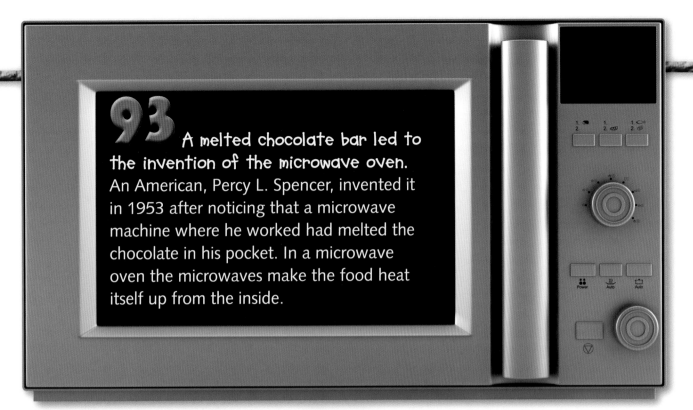

93 A melted chocolate bar led to the invention of the microwave oven. An American, Percy L. Spencer, invented it in 1953 after noticing that a microwave machine where he worked had melted the chocolate in his pocket. In a microwave oven the microwaves make the food heat itself up from the inside.

▲ In a microwave oven the microwaves are deflected by metal vanes down onto the food below.

94 There is no air inside a light bulb. If there was, it would burn out in no time. The first light bulbs failed because air could get in. American Thomas Edison invented an air-tight light bulb in 1879 that could burn for a long time. He opened the first electric light company in 1882.

Vacuum bulb

Filament

◀ In a light bulb, electricity causes a wire filament to glow brightly in the airless bulb.

▲ Energy–saving bulbs make light using fluorescence, where a chemical substance called phosphor lining the tube glows.

Screw thread

Power contact

95 Four thousand years ago in Crete in Greece the king's palaces had flushing toilets. They used rainwater. In England, toilets that flushed when you pulled a handle were invented in the 18th century. In 1885 Thomas Twyford invented the first all-china flushing toilet.

96 Concorde flew at twice the speed of sound, nearly 2150 kilometres an hour. This is at least twice as fast as the earliest jets. The huge jet airliner crossed the Atlantic at a height of over 18,000 metres. All Concordes were retired in 2003.

▼ The Chinese were the first to use gunpowder in war, as in this hand-held gun for firing missiles.

97 Rockets helped the Chinese drive away a Mongol army in the 13th century. The rockets used gunpowder, which the Chinese had invented 300 years earlier, but had only used in fireworks.

98 German war rockets in World War II (1939–1945) could travel 320 kilometres to hit England. They were invented by a scientist called Wernher von Braun. After the war he helped the United States build space rockets.

▼ German rocket pioneer von Braun designed the Saturn V rockets that launched the Apollo astronauts to the Moon. Here he shows an early version to US President Eisenhower.

I DON'T BELIEVE IT!

A 15th-century Chinaman, Wan Hu, tried to make a flying machine out of 47 rockets and two kites. His servants lit all the rockets at the same time, and Wan Hu disappeared forever in a massive explosion.

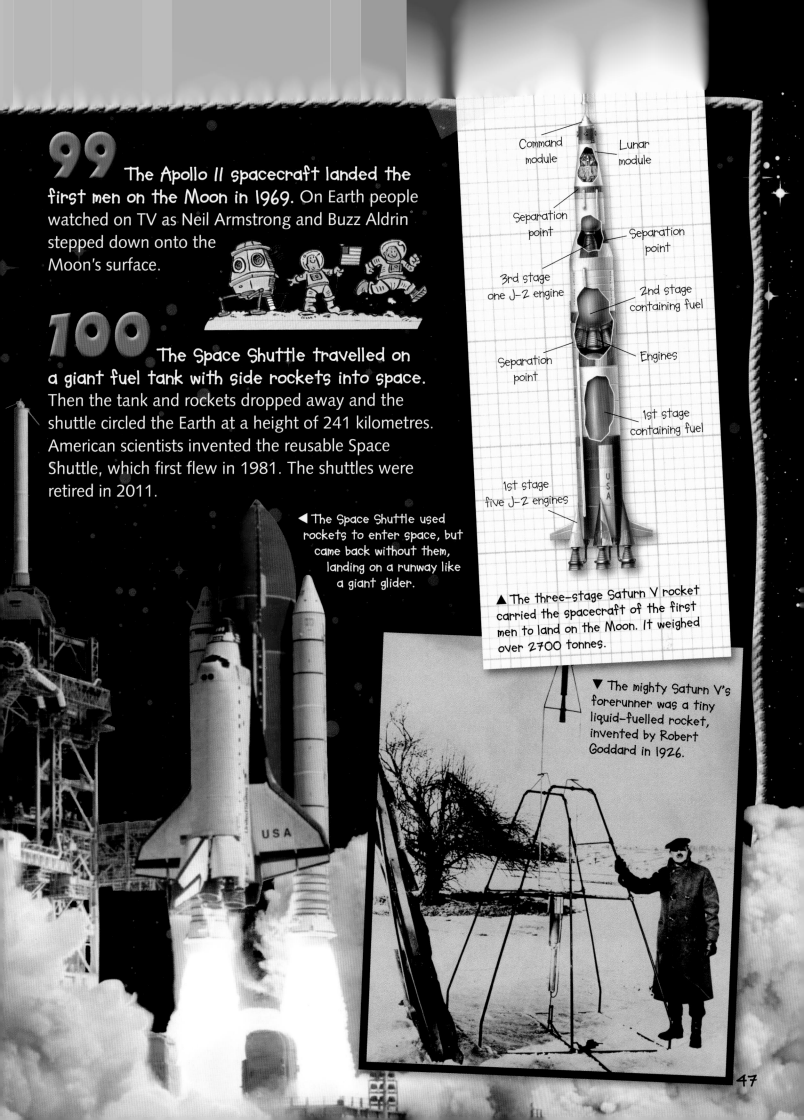

99 The Apollo 11 spacecraft landed the first men on the Moon in 1969. On Earth people watched on TV as Neil Armstrong and Buzz Aldrin stepped down onto the Moon's surface.

100 The Space Shuttle travelled on a giant fuel tank with side rockets into space. Then the tank and rockets dropped away and the shuttle circled the Earth at a height of 241 kilometres. American scientists invented the reusable Space Shuttle, which first flew in 1981. The shuttles were retired in 2011.

◄ The Space Shuttle used rockets to enter space, but came back without them, landing on a runway like a giant glider.

Command module

Lunar module

Separation point

Separation point

3rd stage one J-2 engine

2nd stage containing fuel

Engines

Separation point

1st stage containing fuel

1st stage five J-2 engines

▲ The three-stage Saturn V rocket carried the spacecraft of the first men to land on the Moon. It weighed over 2700 tonnes.

▼ The mighty Saturn V's forerunner was a tiny liquid-fuelled rocket, invented by Robert Goddard in 1926.

Index

Page numbers in **bold** refer to main entries, those in *italics* refer to illustrations